The Science of Faith

Micahyah Meza

Cadmus Publishing
www.cadmuspublishing.com

Copyright © 2022 Micahyah Meza

Published by Cadmus Publishing
www.cadmuspublishing.com
Port Angeles, WA

ISBN: 978-1-63751-343-9

All rights reserved. Copyright under Berne Copyright Convention, Universal Copyright Convention, and Pan-American Copyright Convention. No part of this book may be reproduced, stored in a retrieval system, or transmitted in any form, or by any means, electronic, mechanical, photocopying, recording or otherwise, without prior permission of the author.

Acknowledgments

OFF TOP! First, I must give all the thanks, praise, and glory to the almighty creator YAHWEH and the savior YAHSHUA. HALLELUYAHWEH

In the mighty powerful name of YAHSHUA.

Furthermore, I have to give thanks to my loving, loyal, and beautiful sister, Tisha. Thank you, loved one, and always keep your thoughts bright.

Next, I will give my respect to Meza Sr. and my mother, Susan. Much Love!

Also, much love and respect to Kim, a.k.a. Kimmie.

Nevertheless, much love to K. Michelle Meza and Dandre Jr., you two are a gift to me and I am deeply thankful for you.

Table of Contents

Preface 1
Self-Control 3
The Seed that is Sown 5
Vision Board 7
Creating a Vision Board 9
Self-Talk 11
The Conscious and the Subconscious 15
Speak it into existence 17
Final Note 19
About the Author 20

Preface

This book is infused with life-transforming power. The Science of Faith is summarized and expressed clearly.

Faith is a seed, the word, the thinking, and the vision.

MICAHYAH MEZA

Self-Control

Self-control is the control of one's thoughts, feelings, and actions.

Self-control is a must in order to reach the goals that you have set.

Self-control also strengthens one's mind power.

Having control over what you think about is like having the remote control to the TV. You watch what you want to watch! The thing is, when dealing with the brain and the mental images we watch in our brain if they are watched long enough, they will manifest in our life.

Thoughts become things. Yes, clearly, thoughts become things. Thoughts are also known as Spirits also known as frequencies which are seeds. Seeds, that when sowed, bring forth a harvest.

MICAHYAH MEZA

The Seed that is Sown

The seed that is sown is the thing that grows. If one is not yet clear on what the seed is, then the following information will enlighten you.

The seed is the frequency, the Word, the Vision, the Time, and the money.

Notice, another word that can be used rather than frequency is vibe or mood, so this means one's vibe or mood is a seed.

The thing about the seed is consistency! The seed that is unwavering is the seed that is most likely to become into existence. For example, let us say that every day you think and speak about money in a way of like, respect, and gratitude. Right there, you are sowing a seed.

MICAHYAH MEZA

Vision Board

Having a vision is a must, in the scriptures the book of Proverbs 29:18 reads, "Where there is no vision, the people perish." Notice the word perish can also mean to be lost. Research the websters New World Thesaurus for confirmation about the word, "perish."

Now, with the understanding that people with no vision are or will become lost, it is easy to see that having a vision board is a must.

Being lost, led astray, is living without a profitable purpose.

Creating a vision board is super simple and fun. The vision board will give one a clear picture of the desired goal.

CREATING A VISION BOARD

Use your imagination to make a list of the goals that you want to reach.

Each goal should be a clear vision. For example, if your goal is to get a job, you need to know the job that you want and then write it down.

The next step is to find a picture or take a picture of the job you want and then get a photo album. You can also use an area on a wall in a room where you are regularly in to post the pictures that you took.

Now, that is a simple but brilliant way to create a vision board. Another idea for a vision board is to have the pictures on your phone. Tech has made it so easy to crop in or out.

MICAHYAH MEZA

SELF-TALK

Talking is the communication of information and the information is words or the Word. Reminder, the Word is the seed and so when we self-communicate, we must self-medicate with nourishing words rather than self-hate and toxic words.

Self-communication or self-talk can be viewed as one sowing seed into oneself that will impregnate one's subconscious and then manifest in its season.

Self-talk can also be viewed as affirmations or auto-suggestions, which is a method to keep yourself aligned with the desires you want.

What does toxic self-talk sound like?

Everybody hates me.
I am ugly.
I am stupid.
I am unqualified.
I will never reach my goal.
I am crazy.
I am weak.

What does nourishing self-talk sound like?

I am blessed
I am loved
I am a vessel used to pour love and joy into people's lives.
I am a handsome man or boy.
I am a beautiful woman or girl.
I reach all of my goals
I am extremely successful.
I am strong and have power.

The Conscious and the Subconscious

The best way for me to explain what I have learned about the conscious and the subconscious would be for me to say that they are like a garden. The seeds are pictures, thoughts, and words.

The dominant seeds that are sown are the seeds that will bring forth a harvest.

Therefore, one should focus on the positive at all times.

Think and speak life, success, prosperity, love, joy, and abundant living. Do not allow anyone or anything to sow any toxic information into your garden.

Speak it into existence

Off top, it is a must that I express the idea that the Heavenly Father spoke His creation into existence.

"Then YAHWEH said, 'Let there be light,' and there was light," (Genesis 1:3).

Right there is where you can see that when our Creator speaks His word, it comes into existence.

Key: The breath that He used to speak which has power is the same breath that He put in man when He created man, so that means that man has the power to speak things into existence.

There is power in the tongue that we speak with, so use your words wisely and create life, love, joy, prosperity, and greatness, (Proverbs 18:21).

Final Note

This book was written to enlighten and give the correct knowledge about faith and how to create your faith and walk in it.

Remember, faith is vision, faith is the words one speaks.

Faith is the seed that will come into existence when worked, because faith without works is dead, (James 2:14).

About the Author

    Deep, aware, and tapped in are just a few words that describe Micahyah Meza. A man on his marathon, committed to illuminating the world!

    Micahyah was born in Southern California and has spent the last fifteen years researching and practicing spiritual principles and the practicing of spiritual principles has led to discoveries and results of greatness.

    Therefore, it is only right that the greatness is communicated to the world in the form of the Science of the Faith.

www.ingramcontent.com/pod-product-compliance
Lightning Source LLC
Chambersburg PA
CBHW071918070526
44583CB00016B/2045